Discover the
Winterthur Garden

by Denise Magnani
New Photography by Ray Magnani

Table of Contents

D1240272

"I HAVE ALWAYS LOVED
FLOWERS AND HAD
A GARDEN
AS A CHILD . . .
AND IF YOU HAVE GROWN UP
WITH FLOWERS
AND REALLY SEEN THEM
YOU CAN'T
HELP [BUT] TO HAVE
UNCONSCIOUSLY ABSORBED
AN APPRECIATION
OF PROPORTION, COLOR,
DETAIL,
AND MATERIAL."

Henry Francis du Pont

What Is a Garden?

"*No* doubt about it. The first gardens were not made but discovered," writes Christopher Thacker in *The History of Gardens* (1979). "A natural spot—a clearing in the forest, a valley opening up in a barren mountain-side, an island in a remote lake—made pleasant by a belt of trees, flowering, fragrant, and bearing fruit. The hum of bees mingles with the tinkling fall of water, for a stream winds across the tranquil scene. In the centre there is a grassy space, and the grass is rich with flowers." Like the Garden of Eden and other visions of Paradise, these pleasant places flourished without care.

The oldest pictorial record of a man-made garden comes from ancient Egypt. Now in the British Museum, a small painting dated about 1400 B.C. shows a stone-bordered, rectangular pond filled with fish, waterfowl, lotus blossoms, and reeds. Fruit trees are arranged symmetrically around the pond, and a servant holds a wine jar and a basket of either pomegranates or grapes. Although agriculture surely preceded horticulture, humankind has embraced the growing of plants for pleasure from earliest times.

Throughout history, men, women, and children of every occupation and station in life have created gardens in all possible climates and locales. The greatest have been works of art that perfectly express the spirit of the place and time in which they were made, but even the humblest—a patch of crocus announcing spring or an unnamed rose

1

Henry Francis du Pont

Du Pont opened his museum and garden to the public in 1951.

Left: Italianate stairway at Reflecting Pool.

Fifteenth-Century European Garden

The gardener in this etching tends one of two kinds of flowering plants and seems to have had great success growing fruit on a climbing plant.

blooming by a back gate—also provides moments of grace in the lives of both their owners and passersby.

What should a garden look like? Are there certain plants or ornaments without which a garden cannot hold claim to that title? Philosophers, poets, and garden makers have argued these points for centuries. In *Letter to Appollinaris* (translated by William Melmouth), Pliny the Younger (62–112) described his favorite Tuscan villa. Its garden featured a verdant lawn bordered by a box-wood hedge, fragrant roses and flowering fruit trees, vine-shaded alcoves and cypress topiaries, obelisks, allées, and an exquisite marble summerhouse cooled by a fountain that "rises and instantly disappears." It is remarkable that so many of the details he mentioned appear in gardens created today.

Great garden ideas spread across the globe with each geographical exploration and published report. Every immigrant to a new land brought at least vague notions of what a garden should be. The gardens of one civilization might have been influenced by a hundred others but still possess a spark of originality. Every garden has the potential to be a unique expression of man's relationship with nature, to help us know and appreciate the world in a new way.

The Winterthur Garden feels familiar

even on first
acquaintance.
There are traces
of wildness in the
surrounding
woodlands and
echoes of an agri-
cultural past in
the rolling hills.
Tall canopy trees,
smaller understo-
ry trees, shrubs,
perennials, ferns,
and mosses occur
in layers—as in

the natural landscape. The colors in the garden have been borrowed from the field. One
might imagine oneself in a spot "not made
but discovered."

Look again.

Has an untouched eight-acre eastern
woodland ever come into full bloom in time
for Mother's Day? What natural meadow is
composed only of flowers in colors that are
opposites on the color wheel? Can treelike
rhododendrons native to a Himalayan moun-
tainside appear in Delaware unaided? Perhaps
this is not nature untouched after all. It must
be a garden.

To discover the Winterthur Garden is
to make a journey into the heart of nature, to
enter a realm where we feel in harmony with
the natural world and to find one man's
answer to the age-old question, "What is a
garden?"

Saunders Tree Peony Hybrid

In 536 A.D. a Chinese author identified the original habitat of the wild tree peony, *P. suffruti-cosa*, as eastern Szechuan and Shensi in western China. Gardeners began breeding them, and by 700 A.D. a great many varieties were known.

If You Have Grown Up with Flowers

Trillium grandiflorum
The great white trillium, or wake-robin, is one of the woodland wildflowers that taught du Pont to appreciate "proportion, color, detail, and material."

Left: Henry Francis du Pont, 1887.

Near the end of his life, Henry Francis du Pont said of his beginning, "I was born at Winterthur and I have always loved everything connected with it." Winterthur is located in the foothills of the ancient Appalachian mountain range. The area's gently rolling hills, abundant waterways, and lush vegetation combine to create a landscape of great interest and beauty. The farmland of the piedmont is among the richest in the world and is one of the reasons a tradition of scientific agriculture and interest in botany and ornamental horticulture developed there during colonial times.

Members of the du Pont family emigrated from France to America in 1800 with the intention of establishing a "rural society and commercial enterprise." Eleuthère Irénée du Pont was to be in charge of agriculture, but when the original land development plan failed, Irénée, who had studied chemistry in France, opened a black powder manufactory on the banks of the Brandywine Creek in 1802—E. I. du Pont de Nemours and Company. He named his home and "little farm" at the site Eleutherian Mills. Soon other family members established farm estates of their own on or near the banks of the Brandywine.

A relative described Irénée as a man whose "tastes are simple: botany, hunting, fishing, rural responsibilities. In sum all the joys one can find in country living and in a happy household are his." Although extreme-

5

Family of Gardeners

Pauline and Henry Algernon du Pont encouraged their children to love the natural world. Both Louise and Harry became lifelong gardeners.

ly busy with his new business, he found time to explore his affinity with the natural world. In this he served as a model to his many descendants.

Even with 94 acres at Eleutherian Mills, Irénée needed more land to graze sheep and raise various crops. Over a period of years he purchased 4 additional tracts totaling 444 acres, which became the Winterthur estate when Irénée's daughter Evelina and her husband, Jacques Antoine Bidermann, bought the land and named it after the town of Winterthur, Switzerland, the Bidermanns' ancestral home.

In 1876 Henry Algernon du Pont, Irénée's grandson and a Civil War hero, brought his bride, Mary Pauline, to Winterthur to make a "settled home" in the country. The life they established was full of activity. Pauline, as she was called, managed the household, and her husband took charge of the outdoors, supervising farmwork, felling trees, planting around the house, and laying out roads. Each morning Henry Algernon journeyed the three miles to Eleutherian Mills, where his parents still lived, to work in the company office. Pauline became interested in gardening, and on weekends the young couple happily joined aunts, uncles, cousins, nieces, and nephews in the family habit of "botanizing" in the woods along the Brandywine.

Pauline and Henry Algernon wanted to have a family of their own. Of their seven children, only two survived infancy: Louise, born August 3, 1877, and Henry Francis (called Harry), born May 27, 1880. The two had an idyllic childhood. Winterthur in the late nineteenth century was like a small village with between one hundred and two hundred tenant farmers and their families living and working there, growing crops, erecting houses and farm buildings, and raising animals. Surrounding the agricultural landscape, wildflower-strewn meadows, second-growth forests, ponds, and streams teemed with wildlife. Much later, du Pont recalled that he and Louise had "the run of the place . . . the farm too."

Pauline taught her children to garden in a plot at the end of a path that meandered down a wooded slope east of their house. Henry Algernon believed his children's familiarity with the natural world should also have an intellectual component and required that they learn the Latin names of plants. Many du Pont relatives encouraged the children's burgeoning appreciation of the world around them with birthday gifts of trees and beautiful nature books. With all of this attention, both Louise and Henry Francis became passionate, lifelong gardeners. Of their mother's influence on this devotion, du Pont said simply, "She loved flowers . . . that's the reason I got so interested in them, too."

For young Harry, the idyll abruptly ended in 1893 when at thirteen years of age he was sent to a preparatory academy for boys at Groton, Massachusetts, forty miles

First Garden

To reach their garden plots, Louise and Harry walked down a steep slope that also led to a small greenhouse. Although the site was changed several times over the years, du Pont protected his mother's crab apple (just left of center) until it died of old age in the 1960s.

8

northwest of Boston. A shy and reserved
child, the rigors of an enforced absence from
Winterthur and the seemingly arbitrary rules
that he was required to follow took a heavy
toll. He was extremely homesick, and it did
not help matters when the founder of the
school, the Reverend Endicott Peabody,
demanded that Harry, who was left-handed,
write with his right hand. Not too surprising-
ly, his penmanship never recovered. Louise
and Harry had been educated at home up
until that time (as a girl, Louise was not
expected to leave home). Perhaps no one had
anticipated that Harry would have so much
trouble with spelling and other subjects. He
was imaginative and a visual thinker, but in
1893 accommodations were not generally
made for different learning styles.
Fortunately, he persevered, and before too
long his homesickness lessened a bit,
although his letters home regularly mentioned Winterthur longingly. He was soon
able to report to his parents, "I am beginning
to feel like studying and I hope it will last."

Henry Algernon and Pauline du Pont
were overjoyed when Harry was able to enter
Harvard with advanced standing in 1899.
Two years later he surprised them by request-
ing to enroll at Bussey Institution, Harvard's
college of practical agriculture and horticulture. He seemed to have found a course of
study that conferred an adult's seriousness on
his youthful inclinations. He took courses in
plant identification and care, greenhouse
management, and garden design. He also
immersed himself in the myriad horticultural

opportunities available in Boston and became a frequent visitor at the Arnold Arboretum.

At Harvard, du Pont became reacquainted with Marian Cruger Coffin, a childhood friend of his sister, Louise. From 1900 to 1903, Coffin attended Massachusetts Institute of Technology as a special student because women were not yet admitted to the landscape architecture program. Their mutual interest in horticulture and design formed the basis of a friendship that endured for fifty years and was to have a profound impact on the Winterthur Garden. During their student days, Coffin and du Pont often visited gardens and flower shows together, and after college, with Coffin's mother as a chaperone, they traveled widely to study the great gardens of the world.

Du Pont planned to continue his horticulture studies in graduate school, but after his mother's death, he came home to Winterthur to help his father manage the estate. Thus began a new phase in his life and in the development of Winterthur. Many years later, when questioned about his extraordinary success as a garden artist, his reply left no doubt as to its genesis, "I have always loved flowers and had a garden as a child . . . and if you have grown up with flowers and really seen them you can't help [but] to have unconsciously absorbed an appreciation of proportion, color, detail, and material."

Aster spectabilis
The combination of soft lavender and yellow remained one of du Pont's favorite color combinations.

he entire family was dev-
astated when in 1902 Pauline du Pont
died of cancer at age fifty-eight. Louise
had married Francis B. Crowninshield
and was living in Marblehead,
Massachusetts, so Harry came home to
help manage Winterthur. There was a
great deal of supervisory work to do on the
farm, and the household's management was
quite complicated. Henry Algernon had
become interested in politics (he would serve
as a U.S. senator from Delaware from 1906
to 1917), and his son helped him while they
both tried to become reconciled to their loss.

Just prior to Pauline's death, she and
her husband had enlarged their house and re-
designed the area east of the mansion where
she had taught Louise and Harry to garden
when they were children. The new walled
garden contained lawns, a stone path, foun-
tains, gates, pergolas, twin garden pavilions, a
rectangular water-lily pool, twenty beds for
herbaceous borders, and a rose garden. Partly
to assuage his grief, du Pont planted the new
spaces and experimented with design and
color theories that he had learned in school.
It was perhaps a blessing that the garden was
newly built; he could involve himself in the
activity he had shared with his mother without disturbing anything she had planted.

In the early twentieth century,
American garden writers seemed obsessed
with the topic of color in the garden. This
rage started with English designer and author
Gertrude Jekyll, who had become phenome-

11

Flower Garden

Between 1910 and 1916,
du Pont documented his color
experiments in the formal
flower garden and the "wild garden" in more than four hundred
Lumière autochromes, the first
commercially available color
photographic process. The pink,
white, pale yellow, lavender, and
scarlet color scheme appears in
many subsequent garden
designs.

Left: March Bank.

nally popular since her first book, *Wood and Garden,* was published in 1899. Beautifully written and reprinted many times, it still inspires beginning gardeners. She wrote that one should "try for beauty and harmony everywhere, and especially for harmony of color."

Du Pont read many of Jekyll's books and articles and took it all to heart. In the twenty new planting beds, he conducted countless experiments, trying to achieve the same romantic, harmonious color arrangements of perennials, shrubs, vines, and small, flowering trees that Jekyll described. Yet the light conditions and climate in Delaware differed from those of England, so he was forced to discover his own plant combinations.

Du Pont diligently recorded a wealth of information about his plantings: bloom time, flower color, plant habit, and plant care, for example; and as his schemes grew in complexity, he began keeping notebooks. Within a single notebook he recorded as many as twenty subheadings, a testimony to his attention to the minutest of details.

These flower gardens, the focus of so much painstaking effort, no longer exist. They were removed and replaced with the Louise du Pont Crowninshield Research Building in 1968. But all that du Pont learned about "beauty and harmony" in his horticultural laboratory is still everywhere apparent in the larger landscape at Winterthur.

William Robinson was another British writer whose ideas had a lasting impact on the evolution of the Winterthur

Garden. Shortly after college, du Pont purchased a copy of Robinson's *Wild Garden* (1870). In that seminal work, he advocated growing hardy bulbs and perennials in places "other than the [flower] border" and described this new style as "Winter Aconite flowering under a grove of naked trees in February; by the Snowflake, tall and numerous by the Thames side . . . and by the blue Apennine Anemone staining an English wood blue before the coming of our blue bells."

We may take for granted the notion of creating natural-looking drifts of color beneath trees and shrubs, but in 1902 this was still a revolutionary concept. Du Pont was thrilled by what he read and began his own version by planting a "narcissus grove . . . on a gentle slope where the lawn fades into the woods" northeast of the house. He noted the naturalized daffodils' blooming, just as he recorded everything he observed about the more traditional plantings in the formal flower beds. He started recording what was in bloom in a small notebook during daily walks. The first entry, on February 1, 1902, reads simply, "Scilla." He noted blooming not only in the flower garden and in his "wild garden" but also in the woodlands and meadows. He often wrote suggestions for care and worried over design problems. Mostly, he was concerned with color and sequence of bloom.

Over the years, du Pont's garden experiments expanded; by the 1930s, he was

March Bank

Following William Robinson's lead, du Pont naturalized hundreds of thousands of hardy bulbs and perennials, including the Dutch hybrid crocus and chionodoxa shown here, that would bloom in quick succession from late January through early May. The March Bank is considered to be one of the most successful embodiments of Robinson's theories in the world.

14

First Flowers

Du Pont and his family enjoyed searching for "first flowers"— the earliest harbingers of spring. The diminutive Tommies, or *Crocus tomasinianus,* bloom with snowdrops in February on the March Bank.

keeping track of thousands of plants. He walked at Winterthur every day that he could for the rest of his life. Although his extensive readings in horticultural topics and frequent excursions to study other gardens formed an important part of his continuing education, it was a lifetime of looking and listening to the landscape itself that was the cornerstone upon which he built an artistic triumph. He once explained this in a typically modest statement, "For years I kept records of when the first flowers came out, and I still do as a matter of fact."

Robinson was a proselytizer for the naturalistic garden style and in his zeal was perhaps guilty of downplaying the difficulties of achieving a truly natural look. Du Pont discovered for himself a clever technique of laying out his "wild garden." He was pleased with the drifts of daffodils in his original narcissus grove and decided to extend them to cover the hillside where they grew with thousands of the so-called minor bulbs: snowdrops, winter aconite, snowflakes, adonis, squills, glory-of-the-snow, Italian windflowers, Greek windflowers, crocus, iris, grape-hyacinths, miniature daffodils, species tulips, puschkinia, and many others. To have his garden resemble the way nature plants in colonies or interlocking drifts of flowers, he had gardeners gather bent or crooked sticks, which he arranged to form pleasing organic shapes to outline and enclose a single species of bulb. He decided, "There is nothing better than a branch to give a charming irregularity of contour and still look natural."

Each year, du Pont ordered more and more little bulbs to fit into the wild garden (now called the March Bank)—29,000 in 1909 and 39,000 more in 1910. Bent sticks notwithstanding, squeezing bulbs among tree roots and previously planted bulbs was a herculean task. In 1911 he became ill while in Europe and was unable to supervise that year's planting. He begged his young cousin, Anna Robinson, to stand in for him. The note she wrote says it all: "Dearest Harry—I write in triumph to tell you the bulbs are planted. I have passed sleepless nights at the thought of doing it and now the relief is intense. . . . However, I have decided one thing and that is flowers in their bulbous state are most confusing and that bank is a maze. My admiration for you who evolved it is unbounded."

Having proved himself capable by managing the household for six years, du Pont was given control of the garden and grounds in 1909 while his father was serving in the U.S. Senate. In 1914 he took over the farming operations as well, and in 1916 he married Ruth Wales. When his father died in 1926, Henry Francis du Pont knew that Winterthur and everything connected with it—the garden, farm, and museum—were to be his life's work.

My Work Is in the Garden

*A*lthough du Pont never articulated a formal theory of garden design, we may intuit his methods by opening our hearts and minds to the landscape he created. The Winterthur Garden was a work in progress for more than sixty-five years as du Pont continually evaluated and refined his techniques. The result is a garden of great subtlety that reveals something new on each visit.

Water Lilies

The creator of a naturalistic garden must allow for chance happenings. Water lilies appeared one summer in the stream below the Quarry Garden and have bloomed there ever since.

Naturalism

A defining characteristic of du Pont's work is its basis in a visceral knowledge of the land developed over a lifetime of intimate contact with nature. Landscape architect Julie Moir Meservey observed in *The Inward Garden* (1995), "Any work of art is composed of at least one or a series of *big ideas* . . . that organize your garden into a coherent whole. . . . [and] give structure to your images and unity to the features on your site. Without it, you will not have created a coherent design for your garden." Du Pont's big idea was naturalism, a garden that looks as if it just grew by itself and is in perfect harmony with its site.

The intent of the naturalistic garden is not to deceive anyone into believing that no human created it; rather it celebrates natural beauty and grows from what the designer has learned by observing the natural world. Having grown up on the property, du Pont had an unusual, perhaps unique, perspective

Left: Quarry Garden.

as he formulated his approach. The mysterious woods, shady glens, and open meadows that became the different garden areas were also the archetypal scenes of his childhood. The Winterthur landscape was both the model and canvas for his work of art.

In practical terms, naturalism at Winterthur meant that the paths were curving rather than straight and followed the lay of the land. The paths wound around trees and through plantings that were arranged in layers, evoking an untouched woodland. Native plants were the backbone of the plantings, but exotics (plants native to other locales) were also used if they had the same ecological requirements and looked as if they could have grown naturally at Winterthur.

A naturalistic garden should evolve from site topography and be integrated with it. Du Pont achieved this by distilling and emphasizing the essential character of different portions of his property. Azalea Woods was created in an eight-acre tract of second-growth northeastern forest. Although Japanese Kurume azaleas in luscious colors are most memorable to visitors, it is the magnificent two-hundred-year-old American beeches, white oaks, and tulip-poplars, as well as the rich diversity of woodland shrubs and wild-flowers, that provide the necessary architectural structure for the azaleas. Judicious thinning, pruning, and additions transformed a beloved woods into a spectacularly successful garden.

The Sycamore Area also exemplifies the practice of basing a garden theme on a common roadside scene that usually goes unnoticed. Many gardeners find inspiration in woodlands or stands of wildflowers. Du Pont glorified the stage in forest succession known as an "old-field meadow"—the combination of grasses, wildflowers, shrubs, and small trees that will become a forest. Around a giant sycamore that once shaded grazing cattle, he planted small, flowering trees and rare shrubs, daffodils, and lilies that bloom from April through July.

Sequence of Bloom

Noted landscape architect William H. Frederick, Jr., has written of Winterthur, "The garden is amazing in its complexity and, although seamlessly whole, can best be understood as a series of seasonal garden experiences joined by circulatory paths. In this sense, it is an American version of a Japanese stroll garden. Areas are further joined by a superbly calculated choreography as declining bloom in one area overlaps the beginning of plant interest in another." Du Pont succinctly summed up the incredible focus and the amount of work needed to achieve that floral choreography when he revealed at age eighty-two simply that "I am interested in getting successive bloom in the spring."

The model for a rapidly unfolding bloom sequence was again found in the natural world. From the time he was a child on the Winterthur farm, du Pont was acutely aware of the yearly cycle of birth, death, and rebirth. The Brandywine Valley landscape is spare and brown in winter, the woods silent,

Japanese Maple
The tree and hillside are the same, but the transformation is complete with snowdrops and winter aconite beneath bare branches in February giving way to Virginia bluebells and daffodils under brilliant new April foliage.

cold, and dank through February. But in March, bright green skunk cabbage suddenly emerges in every damp spot.

By late March, the fragrant, bright yellow spicebushes begin blooming, and the forest floor bursts forth in early April before leaves have unfurled on deciduous trees and shrubs. With no foliage to obscure the colors, blue, pink, and white hepatica; yellow trout lily; white toothwort; dutchman's breeches in white tinged with yellow; and palest pink spring beauty teach gardeners all they need to know about making a garden in the woods.

Du Pont created an artistic representation of this sequence on the March Bank when he first imagined his "wild garden" that would bloom in quick succession from late January through June. By using plants that evolved in hot, arid climates, he could push the season, with snowdrops and winter aconite in full bloom before the first native wildflower showed a hint of color.

The Sundial Garden is another example of bloom succession used as an important design strategy. The area (known during du Pont's lifetime as the April Shrub Garden) begins at one end with the earliest magnolias. They are quickly followed by Asian cherries, flowering quince, spirea, viburnums, and crab apples in sequence until, at the opposite end, lilacs bloom beneath lavender princess trees by the end of April. As May progresses, so does the color, as Korean lilacs, viburnums, and fringe trees in the adjacent Sycamore Area come into flower.

No one who has noticed the cavalcade

of color throughout April in the Winterthur Garden will be astonished to find the "once-a-week" path in the Pinetum, where du Pont attempted to add an azalea planting whose flowering proceeded along the path a week at a time. Sometimes, of course, capricious weather foils the scheme.

While the March Bank and the Sundial Garden are the most definitive examples of bloom sequencing, every individual area and the garden as a whole express this idea. Each area has a principal time for most profuse blooming of signature plants, but other species always extend the flowering both before and after in a sort of bell-shape curve of color. Azalea Woods is famous for fullness of bloom by the second week in May, but a great swath of Italian windflowers begin in April, while the architectural Dexter hybrid rhododendrons flower later in May, and Martagon hybrid lilies bloom in June.

Principal actors in the Winterhazel Area are pale yellow *Corylopsis,* or winterhazels, that flower with lavender Korean rhododendrons in April before either has leaves. Even earlier, sometimes by late January, hellebores in cream, mauve, wine, and chartreuse enliven the winter landscape. By the end of April, rhododendron petals have fallen to the earth to set off the vibrant, deep pink blossoms of the tiny, rare *Primula abschasica.*

Martagon Hybrid Lily

Rhododendrons and azaleas thrive in Azalea Woods, with its softly filtered light and acidic soil. Martagon hybrid lilies favor the same conditions and so continue the succession of bloom in Winterthur's woodlands.

When William Frederick described the garden as "a series of seasonal garden experiences joined by circulatory paths," he noted a more critical but elusive aspect of the Winterthur Garden's design. Many gardeners are familiar with the goal to always have something in bloom within a perennial border, but extending this concept to a sixty-acre area is a daunting exercise. On a single visit, it is difficult to apprehend the staggering complexity of the yearly cycle. Superimposed on this overarching yearly pattern are the detailed changes—weekly in spring—within each area. In a garden such as Winterthur's, we are meant to notice and delight in the natural events, both momentous and minute, that occur throughout the year.

Garden Lane in April

Magnificent Sargent cherries along Garden Lane perfectly match the Rhododendron ''Cornell Pink.''This ethereal color composition captures the essence of spring.

Color

As important as naturalism and bloom sequence are to the mood, style, and meaning of the Winterthur Garden, du Pont once admitted that, for him, "color is the thing that really counts more than any other." He had a strong emotional reaction to color, and he wanted his visitors to be as enraptured by it as he was. Once again, it was as a child at Winterthur that he first noticed the power of color to completely transform the landscape with the changing seasons. His notebooks show that through years of close observation on his daily walks, he developed a keen sensitivity to slight nuances of color in plants. It was his patient willingness to experiment over many years, however, that led to the expertise in the use of color evident in the garden.

Du Pont borrowed his palette from the surrounding wild landscape. The soft pastels of spring wildflowers and emergent foliage—white, pink, lavender, blue, yellow, and chartreuse—remained favorites throughout his life. He endlessly combined shades and tints of these colors in the formal flower gardens and in the greater landscape, studying the moods he achieved and the flowers' effects in combination. The quality of light in different seasons and at various times of day profoundly influences perceptions of color, and so he was in agony if other business prevented his evaluation of the changing color schemes.

Du Pont was aware of many theories about color. He called the study "a vast field in itself," but color wheels aside, what really mattered was how the flowers looked in the settings he had in mind. Although expert horticulturists advise against the practice, he had his gardeners move azaleas in full bloom so he could make sure the colors had the desired synergy in the filtered light of a Delaware woodland in May.

Azalea Woods presents a good opportunity to analyze du Pont's use of color. The sequence of bloom begins with bloodroot and violets, native woodland wildflowers that were already growing there. Then in April, the Italian windflower, *Anemone appenina*, forms a delicate pale blue and lavender carpet

Experimenting with Color

Du Pont often paired lavender and cherry red or even scarlet flowers. He believed the colors had a sophisticated and exciting synergy. Lavender *Phlox divaricata* near a cherry red Kurume azalea is just one of the many instances of this color combination in Winterthur's garden.

beneath swelling azalea buds. Soon, more wildflowers join the display—trilliums, Virginia bluebells, and others. There are rare species of azaleas in the garden area, but most are Kurume hybrids from Japan, which are literally smothered in blossoms by mid May. Du Pont favored pastel shades of closely related colors—those adjacent on the color wheel—which give an overall feeling of peace and harmony. Lest eight acres of white, apricot, soft pink, and lavender seem *too* pretty, though, he would add a little spice to the planting or "chic it up," as he said. He planted a lavender azalea next to a scarlet one, a combination that Marian Coffin politely called one of Harry's "near discords" and one he used frequently in later years.

A more commonly used technique to avoid excessive sweetness is to join colors of high contrast, those opposite on the color wheel. The classic example at Winterthur is the Winterhazel Area pairing of cool, greenish-yellow *Corylopsis,* or winterhazel, with the warm lavender Korean rhododendron. Since using contrasting colors side-by-side makes both appear brighter and more intense, basing an entire garden area on this perfectly balanced combination was one of du Pont's most striking and memorable ideas. In some circles, du Pont is more famous for his indoor color work than for his outdoor harmonies.

Twenty years of concentrating on the garden, however, was the prelude to designing the museum's period rooms.

In the garden, the lay of the land and existing trees and shrubs carved the space and provided a structure within which he could work. Inside the museum, his collection of historical rooms and architectural re-creations gave him defined spaces, time periods, and moods to serve as bases for the selection and placement of objects. Placement or arrangement was all important. One of du Pont's oft-quoted interior design maxims was: "If you go into a room, any room, and right away you notice something, it shouldn't be there." Instead of relying on dramatic focal points to give interest, he insisted that the rooms be beautifully balanced ensembles, each piece playing off the others and the whole more important than any of its parts. This approach was an extension of the garden arrangement he had become so adept at composing—lyrical, naturalistic groupings of carefully selected plants that seemed "as if they had always been there." He wanted the rooms to seem "lived in" and for the garden to seem real. In both he downplayed the designer's hand.

Movement

When we approach a garden, the first two decisions we usually make are whether and how to move through it. Historically, relatively few gardens were designed to be experienced by sight alone. Italian Renaissance gardens are often first appreciated from the upper

Artful Paths

Since one must step carefully on the stone pathway in the Quarry Garden, there is an opportunity to stop and smell the flowers.

balcony of a villa; ancient Japanese "dry gardens" (stones set in raked sand) are meditation aids for Zen monks. The pleasure of discovering a garden by walking along its paths, however, is the essence of most garden visits.

A good garden path will entice us to begin a journey and provide enough interest, variety, and comfort along the way to encourage completion. Studies have shown that people generally like to walk in a fairly straight line toward "intermediate destinations," the farthest points along the path that can be seen. As we walk, our intermediate destinations change because the farther we walk, the more we can see. We become bored if the "goals" are more than about two hundred feet apart. When we are in closed places, such as the woods, we are calmed by openings that allow views out. When we are in open spaces, we seem to need partitions that divide large areas into more easily perceived regions. We prefer vistas if we can enjoy them from a protected spot. In any landscape we seek the adventure of lookouts, the mystery of trails, and the comfort of shelter. Du Pont may not have been aware of these behavioral studies, but the path system he created could be a textbook response to the findings. He had walked many miles in gardens and wild places at Winterthur and all over the world and had only to consult his own memories as research.

A vast, roughly elliptical route, today called Garden Lane, circumscribes the house, now Winterthur Museum. It was originally planned as a farm road by Henry Algernon.

In typical fashion, his son retained traces of the past in the landscape and worked from there, designing a complex web of smaller paths off the main road. These subsidiary paths define and traverse the various garden areas and, taken together, help link the sixty intensively planted acres into a unified whole.

In plan, the paths form patterns that, although pleasing, are not fully comprehensible, as an axial or straight system would be. When one is on the paths, however, it becomes obvious that du Pont laid them out in relation to existing landforms, large trees, and rock formations. Throughout the naturalistic areas, the pathways are subtle, harmonious, intimate, never dominant. In du Pont's day, they were grass or bark mulch, though now many have been paved. Trails are cut into the earth slightly, and when seen from below, they seem to disappear, leaving an unbroken view of green.

After du Pont opened his home and garden to the public in 1951, he realized that visitors needed cues to help them decide how to navigate such a large garden. In the early years, during the six weeks of "Spring Tour," du Pont and his head gardener placed green arrows throughout the grounds to point to flowers in bloom. They changed them every few days as the succession of bloom unfolded. As du Pont expanded the garden, he

A Divergent Path

Meandering pathways through Azalea Woods reveal harmonious juxtapositions of color and scale.

View from Oak Hill

A bench provides a comfortable spot from which to survey this spectacular view from Oak Hill. In the foreground, the blooming *Colchicum* species signals that this is an early fall scene.

found it impractical to place arrows in a garden meant to be enjoyed year-round.

Du Pont became adept at suggesting a walking route by merely grouping shrubs to form paths. He subtly invited movement along these "implied paths" by carving openings to many vistas along the way. Some views were of structures or stately trees, but most were of tree or shrub blossoms in colors coordinating or contrasting with those surrounding the visitor on the path. Views of flowers are by nature ephemeral, and du Pont planned dozens of these changing "intermediate destinations" for each area.

When the first garden maps were produced in the 1950s, the names du Pont chose for paths revealed his bias in designing a garden of movement—March Walk, Winterhazel Walk, and Quince Walk. In the Sycamore Area, plantings are arranged along three paths; on Oak Hill, grassy walks lead to spectacular vistas. When we embark upon the paths of the Winterthur Garden, we can only glimpse portions of the road ahead. We are committing ourselves to a journey of discovery.

A Work of Art

In his eighties, du Pont realized that the garden areas he had created during his lifetime were linked by naturalism, sequence of bloom, color, and movement, and he set about strengthening the connections that would unify his work of art. He allowed the river of blue scilla and chionodoxa to flow from the March Bank into Azalea Woods

and down into the Glade Garden. He pruned trees so that the pink at Magnolia Bend could be seen from far up the road amid "Cornell Pink" rhododendrons. In early April, the walk from Magnolia Bend through the Winterhazel Area to the Quarry Garden is a journey laced with yellow from numerous plants. In late April through May, pink runs throughout the entire garden, from an astounding range of flowers, shrubs, and trees. There is still a sense of mystery, but one thing is clear: the whole is beautiful.

Henry Francis du Pont was always able to get to the heart of a matter in a few words. After years of joyful work, he summed up his hope that Winterthur's visitors "may enjoy as I have, not only the flowers, trees, and shrubs, but also the sunlit meadows, shady wood paths, and the peace and great calm of a country place which has been loved and taken care of for three generations."

Quarry Lane

Daffodils and other yellow flowering plants unify the Winterthur Garden with color in early April.

Winterhazel Area

Sometimes an idea is so clear, so compelling, that it silences all disagreement. The combination of winterhazels and Korean rhododendrons may be one of those inimitable garden brainstorms.

Du Pont began planting *Corylopsis* species and *Rhododendron mucronulatum* around 1920, using his father's young Pinetum as an evergreen backdrop. It required considerable faith and foresight to imagine the dense wall of green that the trees would someday become. The colors used— the pale, cool, greenish-yellow of winterhazels and the warm lavender of rhododendron— are precise opposites on the color wheel, the shrubs flowering together before their leaves have appeared. Blooming beneath this perfectly balanced duo are an assortment of perennials whose flower colors are all shades and tints of the principals: hellebores in cream, wine, pink, and chartreuse and *Corydalis bulbosa* in a pale lavender. In 1965, when he was eighty-five, du Pont read about the rare *Primula abschasica* and had to try it. Just as he hoped, its petals matched the rhododendrons. Eureka!

At age eighty-five, du Pont procured the tiny, jewel-like *Primula abschasica* as the final touch for the Winterhazel Area after reading about them in an article by plant expert Lincoln Foster. The addition completed a garden area he had begun thirty years before.

Left: Winterhazel Area.

32

The March Walk entices visitors with sparkling color. Especially after a bleak winter, the vividly colored carpet created by hundreds of thousands of *Scilla siberica* and *Chionodoxa luciliae* is breathtaking.

Ostrich ferns cover the lower banks and valley floor of the March Bank from May through November.

March Bank

The earliest garden area to bloom at Winterthur is also the first one that du Pont created, begun in 1902 when he was twenty-two. The bank is heavily planted with hundreds of thousands of bulbs and herbaceous perennials, most of which bloom and fade before spring foliage unfurls on the trees above.

The mood of this area is anticipation; the first snowdrops *(Galanthus nivalis)* to bloom in January foreshadow spring. In quick succession, golden adonis *(Adonis amurensis),* bright yellow winter aconite *(Eranthis hyemalis),* green-tipped white snowflakes *(Leucojum vernum),* pale lavender *Crocus tomasinianus,* azure glory-of-the-snow *(Chionodoxa luciliae),* and electric blue *Scilla siberica* cover the earth in a gorgeous tapestry. The Virginia bluebell *(Mertensia virginica)* stains the bank blue again in April and May. In July, it is lavender from *Hosta ventricosa,* and throughout summer, the lower banks and valley floor become an essay on texture, carpeted with ostrich ferns that sometimes reach four feet in height. The March Bank anticipates not only spring but also the whole year at Winterthur in this compressed sequence of bloom and naturalism. It was here that du Pont first realized that all of the Winterthur landscape could be his garden.

Pinetum

The Pinetum is a collection of conifers or cone-bearing trees: pines, firs, spruces, cedars, and their relatives. Henry Algernon began it in earnest in 1918 at the urging of his friend Charles Sprague Sargent, first director of the Arnold Arboretum in Jamaica Plain, Massachusetts. Sargent wrote, "I am very much interested in a Pinetum in Delaware . . . one is needed in your region where probably many species can be grown which are not hardy here or near New York." He offered to send the elder du Pont plants if he would "undertake this patriotic work."

In the winter landscape, the Pinetum (seen here in the distance) is a green oasis. As the earth warms and the earliest shrubs and small trees come into flower, the dense evergreens are a backdrop for the fleeting spring blossoms.

In the 1930s and 1940s, du Pont enlivened his father's evergreen planting, adding flowering shrubs to form paths throughout the area: Asian azaleas in every shade of pink, the "once-a-week" path of azaleas meant to change weekly; the deciduous royal azalea, *Rhododendron schlippenbachii,* with incredibly large, pale pink and white flowers that have been likened to butterflies alighting on the branches; and flowering quince. Many shades of red, orange, salmon, pink, and white quince bloom in brilliant counterpoint to somber evergreens in mid April. The Pinetum feels everlasting, "for all time," as du Pont would say, and has become an anchor for the ethereal beauty of the surrounding magnolias, winterhazels, cherries, and quince.

March Walk, Pinetum Walk, Azalea Walk, and Garden Lane converge at Magnolia Bend, where Henry Algernon du Pont planted saucer magnolias around 1880. Here, the Winterthur Garden's past, present, and future coalesce.

Magnolia Bend

On old maps, the "Bend" was where March Walk curved into Garden Lane, and it is still a garden of transition—from the cooling shade of Azalea Woods to the exhilarating openness of the meadow, from spring to summer, and from the past to the present. Records show that the oldest saucer magnolias *(Magnolia x soulangiana)* in this grove were planted around 1880 by Henry Algernon. Henry Francis increased the planting, making the large, pink, chalice-shape blossoms part of a great sweep of pastel color along Garden Lane in April and May.

In recent garden restorations, a beautiful white, blue, and lavender combination has extended the bloom through summer and into fall. Siberian iris, *Viburnum* "Summer Snowflake," white rugosa roses, lavender Russian sage *(Perovskia atriplicifolia),* and the ground cover of electric blue *Ceratostigma plumbaginoides* complement the smooth, gray bark of the magnolias. Fall-blooming lavender *Aster spectabilis* among the other plants echoes the textures of the wildflowers and grasses ripening in the meadow beyond.

Sundial Garden

By 1955 Winterthur had been open nearly four years. Du Pont asked his dear friend landscape architect Marian Coffin to help him design an April garden of flowering shrubs. He wanted it to be "all pink and white," to make April as appealing as May, which is enlivened by Azalea Woods.

The site previously contained tennis and croquet courts and so was quite level, very different from the surrounding rolling topography. Du Pont had recently visited Sissinghurst, the famous garden in England created by Vita Sackville-West and her husband, Sir Harold Nicolson. Nicolson was responsible for planning the architectural spaces enclosed by dense hedges or stone walls that opened onto one another, almost like rooms in a house. Sackville-West, an expert (though self-taught) horticulturist and garden writer, planted the outdoor rooms with voluptuous arrangements of perennials, shrubs, vines, and flowering trees. The style they developed became known as a "room garden."

In Winterthur's version, the Pinetum and an enclosing hedge provided evergreen walls. To furnish the "room," Coffin presented a simple plan featuring fragrant shrubs—magnolias, cherries, quince, crab apples, viburnums, spireas, fothergillas, lilacs, pearlbushes, and roses—and arranged them in concentric circles around an antique armillary sundial. This first garden created expressly for the public was a room made of flowers.

People often ask when is the best time to visit Winterthur's garden. Perhaps it is the day in April when petals drop from *Magnolia* "Wada's Memory" and it appears to snow in the Sundial Garden.

The Sundial Garden, bordered on a side by the Pinetum, is a room made of flowers. A garden bench affords a splendid view of the "furnishings," including lilacs, quince, and cherries.

In Azalea Woods, du Pont choreographed his favored combination of lavender and cherry red, this time with the upright, flame-red torch azalea and woodland phlox and other lavender wildflowers.

Azalea Woods

When the azaleas are in full bloom at Winterthur, usually by the second week of May, more people visit the garden than at any other time of year. It seems ironic that this popular area began with an ecological disaster. In 1904 the chestnut blight, a virulent fungus from the Far East, swept across the eastern seaboard of the United States. The du Ponts had to remove many chestnuts from their property, and by 1912 there were gaping holes in the woodland floors and canopies.

In a bit of serendipity, du Pont happened to visit one of his favorite nurseries, Cottage Gardens Company of Long Island, just after the company had purchased some azaleas that had won a gold medal at the Panama Pacific International Exposition in San Francisco in 1915. They were Kurume hybrid azaleas, named for the city on the Japanese island of Kyushu where Motozo Salamoto originally bred wild forms in 1820. Du Pont bought seventeen plants, not in flower, and placed them in some of the bare spots in the woods not far from the house. He was surprised and delighted the next spring when he discovered that the plants were not only hardy but also covered with blossoms in his favorite colors. Thus began a forty-year odyssey of experimentation with color and plant combinations—experimentation that most declare an unqualified success.

Azalea Woods is a Paradise garden. Eight acres of white flowering dogwoods; hundreds of white, pink, salmon, and red azaleas; Dexter hybrid rhododendrons; and thousands of Spanish bluebells and wildflowers improbably reach full bloom at once. Light softly filters through the towering canopy of American beeches, tulip-poplars, and white oaks; birds sing. Azalea Woods is a garden that proclaims, as poet Robert Browning wrote, "All's right with the world."

Reflecting Pool & Glade Garden

In 1929 du Pont planned an enlargement of his house and commissioned Marian Coffin to redesign the formal garden. Like many landscape architects of the "country house" era, she looked to the great gardens of the Italian Renaissance for inspiration. With its axial symmetry, classical proportions, and refined architectural features, this area is a serene oasis. Coffin's triumph was a grand Italianate staircase leading from the east side of the new wing to a swimming pool, now a reflecting pool filled with water lilies and surrounded by abundant seating furniture, statuary, and container plantings that bloom throughout the summer.

In 1931 du Pont wrote of the rock garden, pools, and waterfalls, "This spring in fact it looked as if they had always been there—so much so that I am simply telling my friends that I had just pulled away the dirt from the existing rock ledge, and what is more, everybody believes it."

Coffin also designed the adjacent Glade Garden, whose naturalistic pools and waterfalls were fashioned from one hundred tons of imported limestone. Originally home to alpine plants, this area is now a shady summer refuge.

The *Encyclopedia Britannica* entry for *peony* begins: "a genus of plants remarkable for their large and gorgeous flowers." Every specimen of herbaceous and tree peonies in the Peony Garden fulfills the definition.

Peony Garden

As part of the 1929 landscaping project, Marian Coffin also designed a path on the west side of the new addition to the mansion and an iris garden that would be visible from Ruth du Pont's bedroom. The garden was a sea of every shade of blue and lavender, which seemed to flow down the hillside. At each end of the path, Coffin placed nineteenth-century garden structures that du Pont had acquired from the Wilmington estate Latimeria. Unfortunately, after several years, a fungus disfigured the iris, and du Pont reluctantly removed them.

In the 1940s, du Pont became interested in preserving the peony hybridization work of Dr. A. P. Saunders. With the help of Saunders's daughter, Silvia, du Pont created a garden that used Coffin's original plan and ornament placement but featured a long-blooming collection of herbaceous and tree peonies in a dazzling range of white, pink, red, yellow, bronze, peach, maroon, and almost black.

Sycamore Area

This garden area is named for a venerable, two-hundred-year-old sycamore that once shaded grazing dairy cows when Winterthur was a working farm (which it was for 150 years). In 1955 du Pont began developing the "good sized area of the alfalfa field east of the Sycamore" with wonderfully fragrant mock-oranges and late-blooming lilacs. When the nearby Sundial Garden began to take shape, he realized that on the hill beyond the giant tree he could continue the succession of bloom into the summer.

This is a display garden, almost like a picture gallery, where visitors walk along grass paths, admiring the May, June, and July flowering trees and shrubs along the way. Three paths converge at the Bristol Summerhouse at the crest of the hill where Winterthur's most peaceful agricultural scenes are visible.

The color scheme is primarily white from mock-oranges *(Philadelphus species),* deutzias, Kousa dogwoods *(Cornus kousa),* fringe trees *(Chionanthus virginicus),* giant dogwoods *(C. controversa),* tree lilacs *(Syringa reticulata), Korean stewartias (Stewartia pseudo-camellia),* and Oyama magnolias *(M. sieboldii);* lavender from Meyer lilacs *(S. meyeri)* and fountain buddleias *(B. alternifolia);* and cherry red from *Weigela* "Eva Rathke" and the ruby horse chestnut *(Aesculus pavia).*

A split-rail fence along the outer edge of the area is decorated by old-fashioned, fragrant pink, white, lavender, and pale yellow climbing roses and gently separates the garden proper from the agricultural setting. Du Pont wanted to preserve the view because it "is a charming one and must be kept permanently as a meadow, as it gives the restful, simple note which I always want Winterthur to have and which no amount of landscaping and planting can improve."

In late June, the Kousa dogwoods in the Sycamore Area are laden with abundant, white starlike blossoms. In the background is the fence that separates the Winterthur Garden from the agricultural landscape.

These fall-blooming *Colchicum* on Oak Hill trumpet one more blast of vibrant color as the summer blooming season gives way to autumn color in the Winterthur Garden.

Oak Hill

Shakespeare said it best: "Ripeness is all." When du Pont began work on Oak Hill, he was eighty years old and wanted to finish his garden. During the last decade of his life, his gardeners worked at a fever pitch, five and a half days a week.

Du Pont had never learned to begin a garden design on paper, as most landscape architects do. He worked intuitively, on-site, both indoors and out. He once commented, "When it comes to arranging furniture, somehow or other, I seem to feel where each piece should go." Garden staff members fondly remember his asking them to stand in certain spots and "be a tree" so he could better visualize form and mass and decide the correct placement of plants. Trees with two-ton root balls were planted during those years, but no specimen was put into the ground until du Pont had personally approved it.

Beneath the graceful scarlet, turkey, and red oaks, a riotous autumn combination of tea viburnums *(V. setigerum)* with hanging clusters of orange fruit, purple beautyberries, (*Callicarpa dichotoma),* and fall-blooming perennials—lavender *Colchicum autumnale,* purple *Crocus sativus,* and bright yellow *Sternbergia lutea*—make a resplendent denouement to three seasons of glorious bloom.

Quarry Garden

The last garden area du Pont developed was one of his most innovative. In 1962, at age eighty-two, he supervised the transformation of an abandoned quarry into a gigantic rock garden. Huge rock slabs were positioned to extend the natural outcroppings, and crevices were planted with a rich assortment of ferns, perennials, and shrubs.

During July and August, vivid native cardinal flowers attract hummingbirds to the Quarry Garden.

In late May and early June, candelabra primroses *(P. x bullesiana and P. bulleyana)* bloom exuberantly from the boggy floor. Du Pont showed his mastery of color one more time: pale orange, pink, lavender, maroon, and soft yellow with a special touch, a tangerine primrose that had to be kept in a greenhouse because it would sometimes "go out" in cold winters. After completing the Quarry Garden, du Pont wrote a tribute to the staff who had helped him create his work of art, the Winterthur Garden: "I am glad that my last gardening and landscaping efforts at Winterthur are closely connected with these men who, during these many years could not have been more obliging and cooperative, and I deeply appreciate their efforts."

*H*enry Francis du Pont never really finished the Winterthur Garden. In 1960, when he was eighty years old, he wrote to a friend, "I am still gardening as actively as ever, and as 25,000 persons come to see the gardens in the six weeks they are open to the public in spring, and are so appreciative, I am doing more and more." During his final trip to England, while visiting gardens, he made copious notes on plants he wanted to try when he got home. Shortly before he died on April 11, 1969, a month shy of eighty-nine years of age, he asked his staff to plant a fringe of white flowering dogwood at the woodland's edge near his golf course. He never saw them bloom.

Du Pont knew it was "useless to lay down too many rules" for after he was gone. He did leave one sign on a path pointing toward the Bristol Summerhouse overlooking the Quarry Garden. It reads:

Keep this view open forever.

H. F. du Pont

Henry Francis du Pont
A diligent recordkeeper, du Pont always carried a notebook during his daily walks in the Winterthur Garden.

Left: View of Bristol Summerhouse.

To learn about Winterthur's Yuletide celebrations, see *Discover Yuletide at Winterthur* by Deborah V. R. Harper.